ENCYCLOPAEDIA BRITANNICA
EDUCATIONAL CORPORATION
310 S. Michigan Avenue • Chicago, Illinois 60604
96106

LEO

♌

July 23 — August 23

Published by Creative Education, Inc., 123 South
Broad Street, Mankato, Minnesota 56001
Copyright© 1989 by Creative Education, Inc.
International copyrights reserved in all countries.
No part of this book may be reproduced in any
form without written permission from the publisher.
Printed in the United States.

Library of Congress Cataloging in Publication Data

Taylor, Paula.
        Leo / Paula Taylor;
        illustrated by Anastasia Mitchell.
            p.   cm.
        Summary: Details the personality traits,
physical appearance, and other characteristics
of individuals born between July 23 and August
23. Lists famous people born under the sign
of Leo.
        ISBN 0-88682-253-X
        1. Leo (Astrology) — Juvenile literature.
[1. Leo (Astrology) 2. Astrology.]
I. Mitchell, Anastasia, ill.   II. Title.
BF1727.35.T39   1989
133.5'2—dc20   89-15699
                                            CIP
                                            AC

Leo

PAULA TAYLOR

Illustrated by
ANASTASIA MITCHELL

CREATIVE EDUCATION INC., MANKATO, MN

If your birthday is between
July 23 and August 23
your sun sign is Leo.
Your key words are "I will."
Your ruler is the Sun.
Your element is fire.
Your symbol is the Lion.
Your energy is fixed.
Your colors are yellow and orange.
Your metal is gold.
Your flower is the poppy.
Your stone is topaz.

In the evening, the noble lion emerges from the shade
of the forest. The King of Beasts haughtily surveys his

domain. His subjects — the striped zebra, the long-legged giraffe, the graceful antelope — watch from a respectful distance, while the lord of the jungle saunters toward the water hole and drinks his fill.

If your sun sign is Leo, you are a born ruler. Like the kingly lion, you take command of any situation simply by being there. When you enter a room, people stop talking and turn to look at you. You may be the shortest person present, but when you draw yourself up to your full height, other people get the feeling they're looking up to you.

Your regal manner immediately sets you apart from others. But it also draws people toward you. Even if you walk into a crowd of strangers, you won't have to go looking for someone to talk to. Other people will naturally cluster around you, and soon you'll have your audience hanging on your every word.

You may only be talking about the weather, but you radiate such warmth and enthusiasm that people are drawn to you. You can talk for five minutes with a stranger and the person will feel as though you've been friends for years.

You can give a speech in front of a hundred people, and each one of them will be convinced that you're talking directly to him or her.

You express your ideas with such conviction that other people believe in them, too. You're the type of person who could persuade a roomful of Democrats to vote Republican.

If you are a Leo, you never do anything halfway. You'll line up on one side or another — you'll never be neutral. Either you'll throw yourself into a project with ferocious intensity or you won't do it at all. Your personal relationships with others will be tumultuous, with frequent ups and downs. You'll either be best friends or bitter enemies. Leos are rarely indifferent.

If you're a Leo, you live life passionately. You feel your emotions intensely and express them with a dramatic flair. You are an actor who assumes many roles. You'll play the parts of a stern taskmaster, a prankster, a diplomat, a child, a carefree vagabond, a wounded lover — all in the space of an hour or two. You could convince someone who's just come in out of the rain that it's a sunny day.

But there's nothing cunning or devious about you. You don't consciously manipulate other people. You simply overwhelm them with your forcefulness and certainty. You sincerely believe you know what's best for people. You assume that everyone wants the things you want and likes the things you like. It never occurs to you that anyone might disagree with you. So

you issue grand pronouncements on almost any subject with the authority of a monarch issuing edicts to loyal subjects. But people rarely resent your advice or orders because your enthusiasm is contagious.

You may not be aware of all the roles you're playing.

But you never forget that you're the star of the show. It's as difficult for you to step out of the spotlight as for a king or queen to give up the throne, but your audience probably won't object to your grandiose manner. They'll be enthralled by your performance — as long as they don't take you as seriously as you take yourself.

There's little danger of that. Even when you're trying to be devious, other people can see right through you. But they probably won't tell you that. They'll like you so much they'll hate to disillusion you.

People will learn to take your passionate outbursts in stride. They'll soon realize that your moods come and go as swiftly as thunderclouds slipping across the sun. One moment you'll be roaring so loudly everyone around you will cringe. Just as suddenly your rage will evaporate, and you'll be contritely begging everyone's forgiveness.

It's impossible for you to hide the way you feel. If you are a Leo, everything you say or do is open and obvious — whether you like it or not. You are so open-hearted and generous that selfish people can easily take advantage of you. You must particularly beware of those who flatter you, as pride is your greatest weakness.

Underneath your self-assurance lurks the fear that other people may not like you. You worry that your audience will turn and walk away, and you will be left alone looking ridiculous. You need plenty of reassurance from people who sincerely appreciate you. But you must not always depend on others for proof of your self-worth. You must also learn to look for sources of emotional strength inside yourself.

Do you recognize yourself? If you were born between July 23 and August 23, you may share most of the personality traits typical of Leo. You probably feel that you don't share all of them. This is not too surprising.

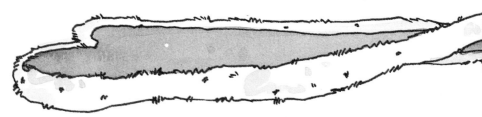

Knowing that someone is a Leo or a Virgo is similar to knowing that he or she is Japanese, Italian, or Egyptian. A person's nationality tells you something about what the person might look like and how he might think and act. Someone who is Irish might have black hair, a round face, and freckles. Someone who is Scottish might be thrifty.

Yet knowing a person's nationality won't tell you everything. Not all people of the same nationality share the same traits. To get a clearer picture of the person, you would have to find out about the person's age, sex, religion, favorite sports, and hobbies.

In the same way, a person's sun sign can provide
some general information, but it cannot reveal all of
the aspects of a personality. If an astrologer wanted to
know more about a person, he or she would have to
find out exactly when and where the person was born.
Then the astrologer would calculate the exact position
of the sun, moon, and the planets of our Solar System
in relation to the earth at the moment of the person's
birth.

Astrologers believe that human beings are affected by
the same energies that cause the sun, moon, and the
planets to move in their orbits. They believe that a
chart showing the position of these heavenly bodies at

the moment of birth can be a kind of blueprint giving
clues to a person's personality and potential.

Drawing up such a chart is no easy matter, since the
earth, as well as the sun, moon, and planets, is
constantly in motion. Because of this movement, even
identical twins born only minutes apart will have
slightly different birth charts, and two Leos whose
birthdays are ten days apart can be very different
indeed.

Interpreting a birth chart is even more complicated
than constructing it. That's why many astrologers
advise beginners to start their study of astrology by

learning about sun signs. Since the sun is the basic supplier of life energy, the sun is a very important factor in a birth chart. Just remember that it is not the only factor.

One more word of caution: it takes approximately twenty-nine days for the sun to move through each of the twelve zones or sun signs of the zodiac. The exact time when the sun passes from one zone to the next varies from year to year, so the dates listed for any sun sign are only approximate.

If you were born on July 23 you might be either Leo or Cancer, and if your birthday is August 23, your sun sign could be Leo or Virgo. In order to tell for sure which you are, you would have to consult an astrological reference book called an ephemeris. After making certain corrections depending on precisely where you were born, you would have to look up your exact time of birth in order to see whether the sun had changed signs by then.

If you were born at one of these turning points and don't have access to an ephemeris, try reading about both signs. See if you can tell which description fits you better.

Your sun sign can't tell you everything about yourself, but it can give some general characteristics. In reading about your sun sign, you may come to know and understand yourself better.

Your Leo Appearance

Your sun sign affects your physical appearance, as well as your personality. Just remember that there are other factors at work, and you probably won't look exactly like this typical Leo portrait.

The typical Leo has:
— an oval face with a ruddy complexion
— steady, dark eyes
— a hooked nose
— a wide mouth
— a firm jaw and chin
— thick hair which is often light-colored and may look wild and untamed
— a large, sturdy build with broad shoulders

The typical Leo:
— stands straight and tall
— moves slowly and deliberately
— speaks and acts decisively
— radiates warmth and charm

What You Might Expect

Your sun sign also affects the way you think and act. As you read the following description of how a Leo might act in certain situations, see if your can recognize yourself. Remember that this is a hypothetical person. Don't look for a mirror image of yourself. You will probably only catch glimpses of the you you know.

School

If you are a Leo, you want everyone to know your name. Each year on the first day of school you want to make sure the teacher knows you. So if you have a new teacher, you'll make a point of arriving in class early. You'll introduce yourself to the teacher and ask if there's anything you can do to help.

By the time the rest of the students wander in, you'll be busy passing out books and paper. When the bell rings, the teacher will let you call the roll and collect information cards. And then you'll be in just the position you wanted — in front of the class. Leos love being the center of attention.

If your teacher is lavish with praise, you may continue in your starring role all year long. You'll be the student who's always prepared and eager to be the first to present your report to the class. You'll be the one who worked both the required math problems and the optional ones. You'll be bursting to volunteer the answers. You'll chair committees and organize field trips.

If a new student enters the class, your teacher will ask you to help the person get acquainted.

Newcomers and old friends alike will be attracted to your warmth and enthusiasm. So will your teachers. In fact, your teachers may be so overwhelmed by your charm that they may give you better grades than you deserve. In that case, you'll probably do only as much work as you need to in order to get by. Leos tend to be a bit lazy.

If you are a typical Leo, you won't read fifty pages if you can get the gist of the story by reading fifteen. If you understand the first three math problems your teacher assigns, you won't bother to do the others. You'll study hard for a test, but you'll hurry through your everyday assignments. Leos are quick to grasp the main point of a story or the outline of an argument, but they get impatient with details.

Your teacher may eventually realize that you aren't working as hard as you should be. Or you may run into a teacher who does not respond to your charms.

Such a teacher expects you to do all the work assigned. In that case, you will probably buckle down and work hard. If you are a Leo, bad grades will be a blow to your pride. You are certain that you are superior to everyone else, and you are anxious to prove it.

If you do the best work you can, you'll expect recognition for it. If your teacher doesn't give you the praise you feel you deserve, you will be deeply wounded. Instead of being the best student in class, you may give up and do nothing at all. You'll distinguish yourself at one end of the spectrum or the other. Leos are never content being mediocre.

If you are denied recognition for your academic talents, you'll seek attention in some other area. One way or another, a Leo will command the spotlight. Since most Leos are natural comics, you'll probably have your fellow students in stitches whenever the teacher's back is turned. And you'll probably find yourself spending most of your time by yourself in the principal's office. Then you'll be miserable. Being an actor isn't any fun without an audience.

Your Leonine dramatic talents may land you a part in the school play. If the dramatics teacher is any judge of acting ability, she'll probably cast you as the star of the show. She'd also do well to put you in charge of promoting it. You'll see that every seat in the house is

filled. There will be posters in every school, church, and grocery store, and announcements will be printed in the newspapers. You'll dream up a skit to advertise the play for the all-school assembly, and you'll get the actors to do short excerpts downtown.

If you're a Leo, you never miss a chance to put on a show. You love wearing costumes — the more outlandish, the better. If the football team needs a mascot to amuse the crowd, you'll be delighted to lead the cheers in a tiger's suit. If there's a Halloween party, you won't just throw on some old scarves and beads

and call yourself a gypsy. You'll come authentically costumed as the Mad Hatter or as the White Rabbit and win first prize.

You probably won't confine your clowning to extracurricular activities. If you're a typical Leo, you'll do nearly everything with a dramatic flair which will alternately amuse and exasperate your teachers. The other students in your woodworking class will obediently practice running the jigsaw through discarded scraps of wood. You, however, will cut a valuable piece of mahogony in two. Instead of making a bird house or a picture frame, you'll be constructing a kayak or a racing car.

In cooking class, you'll chop vegetables with such enthusiasm that you'll nearly chop off your fingers, as well. When you beat cake batter, most of it will end up on the walls and the ceiling. But by the end of the semester, when other students are still trying to soft-boil an egg, you'll be turning out airy souffles and elegant ten-layered tortes. Leos often attempt projects other people consider overly ambitious, but Leos manage to carry them off. Leos believe they can do anything. And they usually can.

Your Leonine self-confidence and enthusiasm make you good at public speaking. Unlike most people, you don't feel nervous standing up in front of the class — you love being the center of attention. You look directly at your audience and speak loudly and clearly.

You get so involved in what you're saying that you rarely even need to refer to your notes.

The teacher never has to tell you to look up from your paper or to stop shuffling your feet. But she may have to remind you that your time is up. You'll be enjoying yourself thoroughly and would be willing to talk for the whole hour.

When your English class is concentrating on grammar and punctuation, you'll arrange to be out in the hall rehearsing a play. When your social studies class is memorizing U.S. presidents, you'll stare out the window. But when it's time for oral reports, you'll come into your own.

If you're a typical Leo, plodding through twenty difficult math problems will probably be torture. Problems that are either right or wrong are not very interesting to you. There's no scope for imagination. Few Leos star in math or science class.

If the band needs a soloist for the spring concert, you'll be the first to audition. If your class is having a talent show, you'll come forward with the finest harmonica solo, the loudest whistle, or the longest pogo stick hop. If you're a Leo, you'll be delighted to show off any kind of skill. What you fear most is being lost in the crowd. Leos hate being ordinary. They'll go to almost any length to distinguish themselves.

Sports and Hobbies

If your sun sign is Leo, you love to perform. It doesn't matter whether you're displaying your skills on the football field, on the high dive, or on the tennis court — as long as someone is watching. If you're a Leo, you don't see the point of exerting yourself if there's no one to applaud. When you make that spectacular flying catch, slice cleanly through the water after a triple somersault, or smash a serve past your opponent, you'll be listening for the roar of approval from the stands.

If you're a Leo, you probably won't become a professional athlete, even though you may have plenty of talent. Leos usually like to play games just for fun. They aren't the sort who willingly submit to a grinding daily routine.

If you're a swimmer and you have an important meet coming up, you'll work out feverishly for many hours a day. When your race comes up, you'll give it all you've got, but then you'll be exhausted. You'll need some time off. You won't be able to face the thought of swimming all the next week. Leos work hard and play hard, but then they need time to rest.

If you are a Leo, you are probably not a very consistent player. You blow hot and cold. If you are up for a baseball game or a tennis match, no one will be able to stop you. But if you're in a slump, almost anyone will play better.

If you're a Leo, you'll be an aggressive player and a tough competitor. You'll take great delight in smashing a hockey puck past the goalie. You'll be thrilled snatching a basketball out of thin air and slamming it through the hoop. But for playful Leos, a game always remains a game. You aren't out to win at any cost. You will play fairly, according to the rules — or not play at all.

There's nothing you'll relish more than a close cross-country race or tennis match, but you won't enjoy a game if the score is too uneven. If you lose by too wide a margin, your pride will suffer — and you'll be equally unhappy if

you win every point. Leos lack the "killer instinct."

Tennis star Evonne Goolagong is a typically warm, cheerful and enthusiastic Leo. She tries her hardest to win, but when she does, she always rushes over to the other side of the net to comfort the loser. Leos are fiercely competitive but rarely ruthless.

Games of strategy and cunning are not for open-hearted, direct Leos. Their moves are usually obvious and apparent to everyone. If you're a friendly Leo, you will probably choose a gregarious sport like bowling, rather than a lonely one like jogging. You'll probably enjoy sports like water-skiing, diving, or gymnastics. These sports will give you a chance to show off your skills.

You may prefer watching games to playing them. Sometimes you may not even feel like watching. Instead of swimming, you may prefer to just lie in the sun. Instead of shussing down the ski slopes, you may spend your vacation in an easy chair by the fire.

When you're feeling lazy, virtually nothing can make you budge. A Leo will sink into a hammock and not emerge for hours — or sit in front of the T.V. all day. If nobody disturbs your reverie, you'll probably fall asleep. Leos are fond of naps.

Except when they're napping, Leos seldom enjoy seclusion. If you're a Leo, you'll probably seek out stimulation, rather than peace and quiet. Your hobbies won't be solitary ones. If you're a gardener, you'll probably start a communal plot. If you're a stamp collector, you'll be president of the stamp club. If you're a mountain climber, you'll hike up the mountain with friends in tow. If you're interested in the arts, you'll join an orchestra or chorus.

Money

If you're a Leo, you probably love spending money, but you never have enough of it. Leos are known for their luxurious tastes. If you're a Leo, you aren't a bargain hunter. You'll go straight to the most expensive store, buy the highest-quality items, and worry about the bill later.

Even if you're not rich, you probably give the impression that you lead a life of luxury. Leos are very conscious of their appearance. You'll probably dress fashionably, even if you

have to do without something else in order to afford nice clothes.

You won't skimp on entertainment. There's nothing a Leo loves more than a party. Through the ages, Leos have been known for their lavish style of entertainment. During the fifteenth century, Lorenzo de Medici entertained the populace of Florence with elaborate masques, pageants, and processions. Another Leo, Louis XIV of France, used his elaborate palace and gardens at Versailles as the setting for dramatic extravaganzas featuring hundreds of costumed nobles. Louis XIV ruled France with such splendor that he became known as the Sun King.

While you will undoubtedly not entertain on as large a scale as Lorenzo de Medici and Louis XIV, you will probably host your parties in just as regal a manner. You won't ask just one friend to dinner when you could invite fifteen or twenty. And you won't serve hamburgers when you could fix filet mignon.

If you go out to lunch with a friend, you won't let your companion pay the bill — you'll grab the check first. Like kings and queens, Leos love to be in the position of dispensing favors to their subjects.

Even if you're broke, you'll probably refuse to accept a friend's offer of a loan. To a proud Leo, admitting the need for help can be humiliating. If a friend asks you for a loan and you don't have the money, you won't say so. You'll be likely to borrow money for your friend from someone else. Leos enjoy providing for others.

Travel

If you're a Leo, you'll probably love traveling — as long as you can go first class. If you have to watch your nickels, you'd rather stay home. If you can afford to travel in style, you'll be off to see the world.

Furthermore, you won't be going on any guided tours. While your fellow travelers dutifully trudge through imposing cathedrals and quaint villages, you'll be

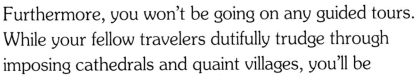

relaxing at a sidewalk cafe. You may miss a few museums in your travels, but you'll manage to visit every notable restaurant and expensive gift shop. By the time you get home, you'll have succeeded in spending every penny.

New Things

If you are a Leo, you find it hard to change your mind. If you've decided to wear red socks, no one will be able to convince you to change to dark blue ones. If you're determined to take biology this semester and the class is full, you'll convince the teacher to let you in, anyway.

Once you've decided to follow a certain path, you'll forge ahead, come what may. If other people try to convince to you deviate from the course you've set, they'll be doomed to failure. Instead, you'll probably convince the rest of the crowd to go your way.

You can easily persuade other people to accept your ideas because you believe in them so strongly. You may or may not have your facts straight, but you speak so authoritatively and argue your case so forcefully that you easily convince people you know what you're talking about.

Your pride can make you obstinate. You will rarely admit to making a mistake. If you get lost in a strange city, you'll refuse to stop for help. You'll insist you know where you're going. You'll continue going in the wrong direction simply because you hate to admit you could make an error. Your stubbornness will exasperate your family and friends.

Your pride will enable you to stand firm in the face of adversity. Leos are known for their nobility and courage. When Jacqueline Kennedy became the first lady, she

was universally admired for her beauty and elegance. Few people suspected the inner strength she exhibited in the days following President Kennedy's death. Throughout the ordeal, Jacqueline Kennedy's brave dignity inspired an entire nation.

You may wonder whether you could face tragedy and despair as bravely as Jacqueline Kennedy. Leos often experience wrenching self-doubts, but when crises occur, almost all Leos respond heroically.

Friends

If your sun sign is Leo, nearly everyone is your friend — even strangers. When you walk down the street, smile at the people you happen to meet — and they will smile back. You'll strike up a conversation with the tired-looking old woman who sits down next to you on the bus. When you get off she'll look fondly after you.

You make a point of asking your neighbor how his sick mother is feeling. You compliment the school secretary on her new sweater. You greet the mailman and the butcher at the supermarket by name. If you're a Leo, you establish an instant rapport with almost everyone.

Leo friendships tend to be stormy. You carry on passionate and intense relationships with other people. If you are someone's friend, you will spend all the time you can spare with that person. You will defend your friend with blind, ferocious loyalty. You will give your friend anything you have.

In return, you will expect your friend to be equally devoted to you. If you feel your friend is neglecting you, your pride will be hurt. Your feelings of love may turn to fury. There will probably be many ups and downs in your relationships.

Instead of accepting your friends as they really are, you may picture them as you would like them to be. Then you feel hurt and angry when they don't live up to all your expectations. Leos are like kings and queens — they like to exercise their royal perogative to command and control others. If you're a Leo, it may be hard for you to admit that you may not necessarily know what's best for another person.

A Leo tends to be egotistical. It's tempting for August-born people to surround themselves with weaker individuals who admire and flatter them. Like monarchs, Leos relish the attention of loyal subjects. Leos also tend to be gullible. They're so open to praise, they don't realize that other people sometimes use them for selfish ends.

Leos with a lust for power can easily become dictators. Some are merely small-scale tyrants who demand loyalty from their family and friends. Others, like Napolean, ruled entire nations with an iron fist in their quest for personal glory and grandeur. Their egos were so monstrous that they considered other people their personal property. Napoleon once remarked that a man as great as he did not care for the lives of a million men. After one battle in which 29,000 died, Napoleon remarked that this was merely "small change."

Yet Napoleon was able to establish a rare rapport with the men he commanded. If you are a Leo, you probably also possess a powerful personal magnetism. With your warmth and charm, you can easily inspire other people to follow you.

If you don't let your pride get in the way, you can achieve true greatness of spirit. You can be like Dag Hammarskjold, who worked unceasingly for equality and peace among all the world's peoples. Dag Hamarskjold attained the position of Secretary General of the United Nations — but he considered himself a "servant of peace." He was killed in a plane crash while trying to arrange a cease fire in the Belgian Congo.

If you are able to concentrate on giving love, rather than receiving it, you will not need to depend on others for your self respect. You will find the greatness you seek inside yourself. As Dag Hammarskjold put it, "The road inwards can become a road outwards."

Health - Rx for Leo

Leo is one of the strongest signs of the zodiac. If you are a Leo, you probably won't suffer from chronic or longlasting illnesses. When you do get sick, you will suddenly get violently ill and probably run a high fever. Then, just as quickly, you'll be feeling fine again. At least that's how you'll insist you'll feel. Leos are proud of their strength and hate to admit any weaknesses. They sometimes insist on getting out of bed before they really should.

Leos tend to live life to the full. They throw themselves, body and soul, into whatever they do. It's hard for them to slow down. If you're a Leo, you probably work long hours and stay up late. You may eat and drink too much.

You should try to get more rest and curb your tendencies toward overwork and overeating. Leo rules

the heart, and hard-driving, emotional August people are particularly prone to heart attacks. To ease the strain on your heart, you should watch your diet and be careful to get enough exercise.

Leos are also prone to emotional heart trouble. If you quarrel with someone, you can look so depressed that your friends will fear you're not long for this world. No one looks more pathetic than a Leo whose pride is hurt. But Leos tend to exaggerate their feelings. Your friends will probably be amazed at how quickly you become your old cheerful self again.

Leo Careers

Like kings and queens, Leos expect to assume a position of authority. No matter what sort of job you choose, you will expect to take command. Your employer will be impressed by your ambition and enthusiasm, but he or she will probably inform you that you need at least a couple of years experience before you take over the company.

If your employer offers to let you start out in sales, you may find yourself directing the operation almost as soon as you had hoped. With a magnetic, persuasive Leo as a member of the sales force, the company's profits should soar.

If you are assigned a routine office job, you will probably be miserable and indignant. You will feel as out of place as a king who finds himself scrubbing the kitchen floor or the queen who suddenly changes places with the housemaid. Leos have little tolerance for dull routine. They feel they're meant for greater things. If you can, you'll delegate the boring jobs to someone else. You'll concentrate on the important work. Leos like to sketch out the broad outlines and let someone else fill in the details.

Leos also need to know that their efforts are recognized and appreciated. A Leo employee who gets plenty of compliments and frequent raises will work tremendously hard. If a raise is out of the question, a Leo will be almost as happy with an impressive title. An August-born person who doesn't feel properly appreciated will soon be looking for another job.

If you are a Leo, you may do well to prepare for some type of work where you can be your own boss. Like kings and queens, Leos love to direct others, but they hate following orders.

If you're a typical Leo, you love to give advice. You would probably make an excellent:

- — psychiatrist
- — psychologist
- — travel agent
- — family counselor
- — business consultant

You also have a knack for fixing things and might do well as a:

- — plumber
- — mechanic
- — repairman

(There's no telling how far you'll go in this sort of field —Henry Ford started out as a watchmaker.)

In business you would do well as any kind of executive or in one of these fields:

- — public relations
- — advertising

Famous Leos

Neil Armstrong, astronaut
Lucille Ball, actress
Ethel Barrymore, actress
Count Basie, jazz musician
Napoleon Bonaparte, French general
Fidel Castro, president of Cuba
Julia Child, author, chef
Lorenzo de Medici, patron of arts
Henry Ford, businessman, inventor
Alfred Hitchcock, movie director, producer
Dustin Hoffman, actor
Mick Jagger, rock singer
Jacqueline Kennedy Onassis, former first lady of U.S.
Benito Mussolini, Italian dictator
Ogden Nash, poet
Linda Ronstadt, singer
Robert Redford, actor
Sir Walter Scott, poet
George Bernard Shaw,
    playwright
Willie Shoemaker, jockey
Sally Struthers, actress
George Wallace, governor of
    Alabama